good deed rain

Taking Her Sides on Immortality

"These late poems recover for us, and—each time I read them—perform anew the complexity of my belovéd first teacher. Brilliant, wounded, tough, generous, determined to see clearly, that man and these poems are necessary to my own sense of the "moral to [our] quaint story. It is threefold: Happiness is love. Love is taking care of what is. The world must not be hateful."

—Scott Cairns
Author of *Slow Pilgrim: The Collected Poems*

"What I find most striking and valuable about Robert Huff's new poems is the drama and immediacy of their tone. Watch the complex way Huff makes beauty and goodness something to be angry about—and anger something to laugh at—so that, at the end of all this mixed emotion, beauty and goodness are more powerful and vivid than they could ever have been if no one got excited about them. Huff's dramatic monologues have a force reminiscent of Shakespeare's; like Shakespeare's, they are dense, intense, and urgent. These are vivid, lively human voices which address us from a heart that is vital and involved. The heart's mood shifts, and shifts again, and gathers energy from every shift, so that those brilliant Huff last lines have the force of bombs."

—Annie Dillard
Author of *Pilgrim at Tinker Creek*

Books by Robert Huff

Colonel Johnson's Ride
    (Wayne State University Press, 1959)
The Course
    (Wayne State University Press, 1966)
The Ventriloquist: New & Selected Poems
    (University of Virginia Press, 1977)
Shore Guide to Flocking Names
    (Fanferon Press, 1985)
Taking Her Sides on Immortality
    (Good Deed Rain, 2019)

TAKING HER SIDES ON IMMORTALITY

Poems by

ROBERT HUFF

Good Deed Rain ◊ Bellingham, Washington ◊ 2019

Taking Her Sides on Immortality © 2019
Good Deed Rain, Bellingham, WA.
ISBN 978-1-64516-989-5

Writing: Robert Huff
Introduction: Samuel Green
Cover Painting: Ursula McCabe
Author Cover Photo: courtesy of Ursula McCabe
Cover Production: Fred Sodt
Editor: Allen Frost
"Auld Lang Syne" courtesy of WWU Special Collections
    Library, Bellingham, WA.

Acknowledgments:

To the editors of the following publications in which these poems first appeared, the author makes grateful acknowledgment:

Chicago Tribune Sunday Magazine: "A Posthumous Exhibition of the Art of
    Robert Huck"
The North American Review: "The Pact"
The Ohio Review: "Rose of His World"
Jeopardy: "Hit Dirge from a Flop"
The Niagara Review: "Passing Through"
Poetry: "Lines for William Golding," "While the Now Generation Basks in
    its Brand New Milky Way" and "Auld Lang Syne"
Oregon East: Theodore Roethke Memorial Issue: "Spirit Duck"
The Mid-American Review: "A Fetish for Molly," "MacKenzie Bridge"
The Bellingham Herald Friday Magazine: "A Sandwich for Celina Near a Rest
    Stop in California"
Poetry Now: "On the Morning of the Death of Robert Hillyer," "Boy in
    the Suburbs" and "For a Man Who Died Quickly on a Road in
    Mexico"
Carolina Quarterly: "Ushers," "April 3, 1978"
Western Humanities Review: "Taking Her Sides on Immortality"

To Margaret

INTRODUCTION

MY FIRST CONTACT WITH ROBERT HUFF came in the spring of 1972, at what was then Western Washington State College (it's Western Washington University now) when I asked him to be an adviser for my honors thesis. I had read and studied his two collections, *Colonel Johnson's Ride* and *The Course*, and admired them. Because I was a transfer student from a community college, Bob didn't know me, so he asked me to bring him some poems to look at before he made his decision. My thesis proposal was for a collection of sonnets, so I brought him half a dozen. He was unimpressed: "You are not John Donne. Stop trying to write like your version of him." He wanted to know what my own voice was like, so he gave me some specific assignments and asked me to bring in four non-sonnets. When I delivered them, a few days later, he said, "Now that's more like it! We can work with this." He agreed to be one of my advisers if I'd abandon the sonnet sequence idea and learn how to find my own way. He wanted me to wait and learn my craft better before trying something so important as a good sonnet. Looking back from more than 45 years, I know that if I have found my own way, it was in large part because of my old teacher's early guidance and example. Bob taught for more than twenty-five years. I'm just one of the many students to whom he was generous with his time. It was agreed between us that poetry is serious business and worthy of giving one's life to. I owe him.

Born in 1924, Robert Huff was one of that magic generation of poets whose ranks included Donald Justice, Richard Wilbur, James Dickey, Denise Levertov, Anthony Hecht, Alan Dugan, Richard Hugo, Anne Sexton, John Haines, Donald Hall, Robert Bly, Marie Ponsot, Philip Levine, James Wright, Adrienne Rich, Galway Kinnell,

Carolyn Kizer, Hayden Carruth, Lisel Mueller, and more than a hundred others without whom the face of poetry today would be unrecognizable. Many of them were his friends, and reviews of his books showed that his own work as a poet was well-respected. Anthony Hecht admired " . . . the language exploding into articulations as if to say, 'And I only am escaped alone to tell thee'." James Wright said, "When I first read a few poems by Robert Huff I was startled by their bounce, their comedy, their depth of feeling—by their general artistic authority." Not only was Bob one of the best-read poets I've ever encountered, but he kept up on practicing painters and composers. He loved and understood jazz in all its incarnations. An avid hunter and fisherman in his youth, he became a composed and patient birdwatcher as he aged, spending (as he said) a lot of time sitting on beaches, the banks of streams and lakes, just watching. Like many of his contemporaries, he was also a veteran of WWII, having served in the European theater, and having survived when his bomber was shot down in combat.

After winning the AWP prize for his third book, *The Ventriloquist: New & Selected Poems*, in 1977, Bob didn't publish another volume for eight years, when a finely printed chapbook, *Shore Guide to Flocking Birds*, appeared from a small press. He was never in a hurry to publish. Though he wrote constantly, he was an obsessive reviser. His poems still appeared in good magazines, and he gave readings in university-sponsored reading programs by invitation.

Only a few years after his retirement from Western, Bob died in a house fire at the age of sixty-nine. Though there were rumors that he had left behind a completed unpublished book manuscript, circumstances were such that no one seemed able to track it down. However, the rumor of its existence would not completely go away, and old students of Bob's would periodically talk among themselves about the possibility of discovery. It was only in 2018 that a forgotten typescript of *Taking Her Sides on Immortality* finally surfaced among some papers belonging to Bob's artist daughter, Ursula. Though it took some months to gain the proper legal permissions, enough readers had faith in the manuscript to persevere, and Allen Frost agreed to bring out an edition of the finished book with a cover illustration by Ursula.

In this age when the personality of the poet and the popular spectacle of presentation too often seem to be more important than the potential lasting nature of the poems themselves, why should it matter that these "lost" poems by Robert Huff find an audience nearly twenty-five years after the poet's death? Bob himself would be surprised at the question if it regarded a poet other than himself. Though he had a reverence for certain poets—Yeats, Roethke, Bishop, Dylan Thomas (his son is named after Thomas), James Wright—it was their poems he went to, over and over again. And the poems in *Taking Her Sides on Immortality* transcend their time of making.

When I was a graduate student in the WWU English Department, still working with Bob whenever I could, I read hundreds of books, beginning the process of licking away at the huge glacier of poetry that came before. Roethke was a poet Bob very much admired, and he was a favorite of mine, as well. I remember reading Roethke's poem, "Where Knock Is Open Wide," and having the sudden feeling that I should recognize the title from somewhere. My first thought was Dickinson, but I couldn't place it. This was in pre-Google days, remember, so I had to do it the hard way: I began at page one of Thomas Johnson's wonderful collection of Dickinson's *Complete Poems*, and read through the entire thing. No luck, but I was still convinced the title was a quote from somewhere. I went to my favorite professors in the department and explained my problem. None of them seemed very interested. Finally Bob came in to work. "Why are you so down?" he asked. I told him about being troubled by Roethke's title. "Ah," he said. "That's from Christopher Smart, 'Song of David,' lines . . . 460-62, I think." Then he quoted them:

And in the seat to faith assign'd,
Where ask is have, where seek is find,
Where knock is open wide.

He had tears in his eyes when he finished. At the time I didn't know why, but now I think I do. From great human need, we lower ourselves into the sometimes uncomfortable seat of faith in poetry, having done the often difficult work of opening ourselves to what might be there. These new poems are worth that faith. They invite us in.

Samuel Green
Inaugural Poet Laureate, Washington State

CONTENTS

Documentary..23
Mallard Dying..24
The Spirit of Grandmère Fontaine...............................26
A Country Tale..28
Nocturnal Invocation in October..................................32
Taking Her Sides on Immortality..................................34
Auld Lang Syne...38
A Posthumous Exhibition of the Art of Robert Huck....40
Ushers...41
A Sandwich for Celina by a Spring Near a Rest Stop in
    California...42
Aboard the Old *New Wales*..43
Just Lucky, I Guess..45
For a Man Who Died Quickly on a Road in Mexico.....46
Concerning Poetry..47
On the Morning of the Death of Robert Hillyer...........48
Trio: A Fable..49
April 3, 1978..51
Lines for William Golding...52
One Sober May 18th in 1980..54
Kelly Scannell Echoes at Yellowstone...........................56
While the New Generation Basks in Its Brand New Milky
    Way..58
Hallelujah..60
Carried Away...61
Watching Heartthrobs Engage the Strait of Georgia......62
The Hearing..64
Back Yard Patrolled by Blue Jays in the Bare Year,
    1980..65

Hit Dirge from a Flop...66
Rock Music Sara Made Me in Bermuda...........................67
Kemo Sabe...68
Centerfold Copy for the Girl Next Door...........................69
Assay in Rhyme..70
A Fetish for Molly..77
As the Mirror on New Year's Day.......................................78
Historical May Day, 1968..79
The Crossing: A Short Story..80
Margaret as a Still Lifesaver...83
Will Rogers Says to Wiley Post...84
Girl of Their Dreams...85
In Memory of Wilfred Owen..88
With Albert Pinkham Ryder on a Bay in Puget Sound..89
Passing Through..90
Rose of His World..91
A Gentle Warning to God's Brave Swan Willow............92
The Pact..93
Clare de Lune..94
Municipal Park...95
Found Bottled in a Tide Pool Near Lincoln City, Oregon,
    Addressed to M. S. B. 96
Postscript...97
Boy in the Suburbs...98
MacKenzie Bridge..99
Gravestone Inscription...100
Late Show..101
Spirit Duck..102

*We love things which disappear
and are found
creatures who plummet
and become . . .*

        "Proust in the Waters"
        —Michael Ondaatje

DOCUMENTARY

In Memory of James Wright

The day we flushed the woodcock with Buren,
Mild brother of untouchable Lucille
Osterberg, her line was busy, and it
Wasn't bleak March, by God, this lean year, Jim,
Nor was it St. Paul then or Hunter College.
It was my dear old homey Michigan.
Was rabbit country, fairly good for birds,
For fuzzy kids with .22's and BB
Guns and double-barrels—as skittish as today—
Which we damned well guessed had a lot to do
With torch songs, Sandburg, early Hemingway,
World War I, rum runners, Valentino . . .

Vast dream herds, far off, grazing in Wyoming, . . .

Damp copper mines old uncles bragged about
When they got liquored up poetical,
Squirrel hunters crouched in dying chestnut groves,
Some bolder gunners over in Chicago
Framing connections with cold neighborhoods.
So you had to get set to leave Ohio.
I had to prove out quick for Lucille's brother,
Whose boyish heart, I'm sure, was busy too.
The Lake was icing, hunting really lousy,
But maple leaves turned twisting wonderful.
I dreamed transformed Lucille kept our grim kind
Downy and close to her sweet pins and feathers.

MALLARD DYING

I am preoccupied with how I'm trying
To stay alive by dwelling on my dying
Of a wing-shot's faulty swing. Amen. Not flying.

Body becoming prematurely old,
I feel the wretched fading of my bold
Blood sun-fetched still into an arctic cold.

After I got intoxicated, fraught
With lead shot, chilled, I found grim pain for thought,
And, though it really hurt, I thought a lot

About my roles as stud and work of art.
Poisoned by chance, my being sensed some part
Of that dawn hunter's jumbled human heart.

I shared a little gale with him; the rain
That wracked my wing bones whipped about his brain;
One of his eyes ran like a windowpane

Until I got a vision of his life
Before his near miss punctured like a knife.
Complete with lovers, offspring, and blond wife.

Most times artistic with a scatter gun,
He adored women, sired a bastard son;
Believed in clean kills, hated what he'd done;

Became part of my memory; must linger,
Camouflaged icon of Our-Bad-Luck-Bringer,
My pulse aflutter in his trigger finger,

Till we're out of my focus, and I go
Back to a yolk-like yearning, fuzzy, slow,
Within which I believe I'm sure to know

The nature of my migratory beams
Led to this gunner's delta's fanning streams
Shaping us out of his and my gods' dreams.

THE SPIRIT OF GRANDMÈRE FONTAINE

Belle habitante—Lo, shapely teenage ghost,
Shade in my dwarf-Sahara-dazzled mind . . .
I would be active too, a slimmer host,
Less taken by surprise, trim, toward refined,

Cordial, and not so utterly enthralled,
Had some kind aunt blessed me with one tintype
Of her at sweet sixteen in lace, posed, called
On to look not quite prim but less, well, ripe.

Last time she popped in (pushing eighty-four?),
Wheeling her bandaged eyes around a tree,
All keyed up, rolled on through the locked Dutch door
Rambling about her recent surgery,

I recognized all of her right away,
Glad she was brave enough to see suns slide
Between the glossy maples, watch them sway
Into translucent leaves before she died.

Flushed now, long chestnut locks askew, each curl
A little startled, bridal negligee
Touchingly hip-shot: Grandmère, gleaming girl
Trueborn Canucks would glop at any day,

Assures me her boy-groom is fast asleep,
Talks of an urge, a timeless sense of reeling
My way because a promise is to keep,
her fears about how I might not be feeling.

Remember when, she smiles, that pretty wife
Of yours told you a seedy antique dealer
Hounded her through his shop as if dear life
Depended on a touch, knelt down to feel her,

Crying: Sweet girl, your being in this room
Puts all my dreams together in new light.
Grandson, believe me here beyond my tomb,
Truth took that lecher's tongue. Yes. He was right.

She colors. Oh, dear yes—Regarding Light,
Perhaps a few more helpful thoughts to say
Anent such passion morning, noon, and night:
Yeats' silver apples purely gold by day,

Vermeer, nocturnal Albert Pinkham Ryder,
That glaze it puts upon wet bark and wings
(Upon the eyes of him who knelt beside her).
It brings much heart-felt grace to little things.

On which she blows a kiss, lips fluttering.
Gracing the small, she whispers. See you soon.
Thus fading toward her sweetheart's matching ring,
Thread spooled, pins, thimbles, and her patron moon.

A COUNTRY TALE

The infant baby Orville
You could squeeze and chuck and pinch,
But he wailed against his daddy,
Cleaving to his mama's finch,

Was attracted to the sand fleas
Carpet-nested on the floor
And the mice his mother worried,
And he grew and called Or,

Who murmured at the marmots
And whistled to the wrens,
A stump-farm roly-poly
Rubbing up against the pens,

Where he lullabied the farrows,
Gossiped with the doting sows,
Fairytaled tearful free-martins,
Mimed soap operas for the cows.

Orville grew and barked his coppers,
Barked a tune back to his dog,
Bought himself a green jalopy,
Dubbed the flivver Coughing Frog.

Lo, it sputtered to the village,
And it hacked him off to school,
Where he sighed behind blond Dory
When he wasn't on the stool

In the corner, where Miss Troutman
Made him wear a pointed cap
For humming to a field mouse
He had cradled in his lap,

For chortling to the pigeons
In three incubating eggs
A ditty Or intended
To put waltzing in their legs,

For joining, a cappella,
Several starlings in the yard—
Much deplored by grim Miss Troutman,
Who declared Or's case was hard.

Bug Buren was a bully
Whose eyes were almost blue,
Both of which pawed pretty Dory.
Buren's daydreams nightmare, too,

Till his inner eye throbbed daily
And one outer found a tic
Had control to wink him heady
When his tongue felt tanned and thick.

Orville loved his bouncy flivver,
Which he'd nicknamed Coughing Frog,
Sometimes even though it lonesome
For coot, tule, polliwog,

For the damselfly of August,
For the sleepy winter hugs
Of the deep lake mud of winter.
Or was fond of taking chugs

In C. F. in bleak December
Through the hills around the lake,
Where he'd once discovered Dory
With a sunning garter snake,

Looking blond and quick and charming
As a goldfinch. Or could tell
She was crooning to the creature
Clearly as a vesper bell.

Oh, Or often pictured Dory
Singing to that summer snake
As he chugged between the snow drifts
Heaped around the river's lake—

Which is just what he was doing
On the night he spied her small
Naked figure nearly frozen,
Curled up like an animal,

Barely breathing, in a wind-blown
Flimsy blanket of new snow.
Oh, Or wrapped her in his jacket,
Rubbed, wept, put the Frog in low,

Knew they had to risk a short cut
For her dear life's fragile sake,
Plowed across a snowy meadow,
Churned onto the frozen lake.

Chanting to the mute swan's silence,
To the snowy owl's wide wings,
Near the halfway of their crossing,
Calling out for small blessings,

Or outsang a sudden snapping
In the air mid-channel twice—
Then a snarled crack-crack, a sliding
Toward a black gap as the ice

Gave way, and they were settling
Through a tunnel in an ear
That heard absolutely nothing
perfectly and loud and clear.

It explained no swift connections
In a world of come and go,
Nor celebrated asters
Nor accounted for the snow

Nor echoed any coda:
Only something like a bell
That glittered for the crappies
And the drowsy pickerel

Was tongueless and as steady
As the tic in Buren's eye
Or an osprey while it's diving,
And it could not grow or try

One newborn sound for Orville,
Known as Or for his song's sake,
Who drowned embracing Dory,
Who once charmed a garter snake.

Nothing, not like any warbler,
In that tunnel or that bell,
Whistling, where there's nothing warm
To talk about or tell.

NOCTURNAL INVOCATION IN OCTOBER

—To M. S. B.

Like Lanier even and the least of us,
I must talk more these days to sanderlings,
Curley, reed, rail, the windy coastal rose,
Late, cornered weavers settling for confusion,
Twilight translucent in an alder grove,
This tidal inlet following the moon.

Less giving than to Ryder or Redon,
Love never looked my fingers in the eye.
The kiss I gave back to the Blarney stone,
As touching as it was indelicate,
Stirs my imagination still, alas,
Its tongue in any language sensual.

So kiting here the tail end of my tune,
A little loony, too, I ask: Small bay,
Kind miniature, how goes your silver weather?
Confronted with this nightscape autumn dream—
Time without question grimly winging it—
What does the goat hawk tell, mild chuck-will's-widow,

The barred owl say about our assignation?
No wee Byronic cantos from these birds?
No cricket chirps this Oriental scene?
Our tryst unnoted by the whip-poor-will?
I'd like an echo of the nightingale
Bounced by a mockingbird in Arkansas

Once more, albeit pure colonial.
Inlet, I'd like to know you're listening
To these sweet nothings not all wasted here.
Tell me the moon's rub likes my midnight oil,
You're moved to rescue me from rock and roll,
Buoy me beyond earshot of Nashville noises,

And be a musey mistress to this soul,
Whose S-O-S itself these nights forgetful
Signals its fear of whistling in the dark,
A fear you'll ripple off without a try
At sending back one sign of water music—
That lonesome lunar sound. O careless love,

Your tender airlift lilting, tune us in,
Tune all of us night birds toward unison:
Limpkins, nightjars, owls barned, saw-whets and barreds,
Great downy grays, vast snowies, boreals,
Until the herons roosting in this cove
Flock cozy autumn dreams, O careless love.

TAKING HER SIDES ON IMMORTALITY
March 30, 1979

*A Breathing Woman
Yesterday—Endowed with Paradise.*

Miss Lukow, who had never been pregnant
Or evacuated from Three Mile Island,
Didn't know she had preyed on John Crowe Ransom's mind,
Was fondly recreated by that man,
And whelped, aged forty, in Saint Louis, Mo.
Swaddled in cozy silhouettes between two
Migrating Steller's jays near the squirming glad
Of T. S. Eliot's favorite maple trees.
Being again did make her blue and cagey
About mankind, stray dogs, roses, and sex,
Which, yonder her prim thighs, fizzed in the air,
Failing, she minced, and fiddling with the lilacs.
Young folks, she guessed, were flowery girls and boys
Or bitchy partners sparring in a ring—
Had liked such lines once—Why? Spoiled Amherst kids
Were mindless twits. Miss Lukow seemed to see
Language like leafy ears on every tree.

Well, well, John Crowe's newborn sighed, towns like this
Might brew fine beer and frown on privacy,
Build Catholic schools, and bake bone's crimson chime
Into a dread of August every summer.
Great cool lakes, she foresaw, gloved Lower Michigan,
Mittening up one's thumb and index finger.
So off she went, for in her purse she found
A pen and cash enough to buy a 1936
Pea-green, restored LaSalle, which the Almighty
Had forgotten to tell John Crowe to teach
Her how to drive. In the garage therefore
Was her chauffeur, buttoning up his collar

Like a studied, black-tied gigolo on the prance,
Arabian enough to light up a Camel
And bareback dreams on humpbacked, twisty roads
Until Miss Lukow's oxfords toed the sand
Beside that River trombone out of time
Long before Glenn Miller vanished in grave fog
Or early natives of old Saugatuck
Named it the K-A-L-A-M-A-Z-
O—Oh, what a float that Kalamazoo!

John claimed that he recalled when she arrived
It looked like Tennessee. A great blue heron
Lifted himself, with her bright spirit light
In his lanky care as any lively minnow,
Out of Bug Slough and kited for the Lake
Almost as if dear hopefully articulate
Miss Lukow, clearly touched by Missikamaa,
Hosted by an Aptitude for Bird,
Was soaring toward the Gulf of Mexico—
Calling a pied-billed grebe a canvasback,
A bufflehead a wigeon, and a hooded
Merganser anything but a pintail
Or a tree duck or that silly sparrow hawk
Balancing small twigs like a miniature
Eagle on lookout for motion gamy,
Fuzzy, warm, or cold as Atlantic salmon.
She couldn't tell when she'd got so enthused—
Calling, counting on Orphic tongue, to claim
The reappearing eye of Audubon.
Casting eccentric light on classy wings,
Carefully spare as Isak Dinesen,
For birds, Miss Lukow called, for animals.

Her green ears tippled at the April air.
Sweet virginal, she sang, immortal waves
Lave my old fears away. God's new again.

Blessed are dogfish and Christian Scientists.
This vision tangles time. I feel surprise
Indeed. And so she did, for on the beach
A mushroom cloud emitted primal noise,
Cleared to reveal one smoky drummer boy
And three guitars nimbused in savage hair.
Thank innocence, Miss Lukow did not know
The lead guitarist of these mangy crackers
Was an Irish aristocrat named Christopher,
Born in a castle, sent to Oxford yet,
Who talked a lot like Auden when offstage.
Nor had John Crowe conceived this haloed happening:
Amplified twang, eight beaten target eyes
In concert, one frightened lady gaping
At bass drum's bold-faced sign—PAP O HUCK FINN.
What can such volume mean, she cried, reeling
As if the Great Lake's undertow vibrated
All about her in the shocked and trembling air.

Her strange voice managed: Lord, if this is hell,
Forgive my make-believe. Another time
I played at girlish boyhood with a snake,
Garter, most gentle creature. Mistaken.
Maybe I clocked around too much with rhyme—
But didn't I send your driver back home quick?
I am beholden to divine control.
For Love's sake, how long have I lain alone?
As for Missouri, Amherst, deep South, here,
Never was catty, Sir. you must know why
Fear of my fellow was Your constant purr.
Now we've been brought together, I believe
Your rock contains our rolling All around.
I would be pristine, folksy, but this echoing,
Repeated blam pops in my inner ear
An ache uncommonly hysterical.

Light plays with shade, the prayerful say, and ghosts
May intervene. Sound John Crowe, dipped in shadows
Of sage beads strung for quaint ladies, hearing hers
Bell-clear and blue beyond Miss Lukow's time,
Swelled his thin voice up to the troubled sky:
Retrieve. Return Perfection to her mound.

AULD LANG SYNE

When I see Aphrodite's locks
Curled above Mae's glad rags—
Especially when Mae's elbowing
Between two crying jags

And Joe behind the bar can tell
How long she'll bawl and beg
Before she smears my handkerchief,
Perks up, pats at my leg,

Whispers aloud: "Only as old
As what the heart reveals . . ."
I know if we have one more Scotch
I'll slip back where it feels

Autumnal on the campus, green
To orange, rust, a psalm
Hovering in the elms which shade
Professor L. Kirschbaum,

Who waddled into Annex A
That post-war, amber year
Platoons of wrinkled freshmen troops
Signed up to read Shakespeare

And found Professor Leo set
The Quonset hut aglow
To illustrate that pound for pound,
Pricked, prime tongue's heady flow

Sizes the blood more cuttingly
Than beans picked row by row.
Thus he compared Avon's sweet bard
To Walden Pond's Thoreau.

Round Leo Kirschbaum's is the kind
Of memory one keeps.
In time with Hopkins' tearful child,
I listen. Leo weeps

For Hector's fate, for Antony's,
The grief of aged Lear;
For Sam, who fell for altitude
And failed to soar, Sam's tear.

For Leo I shall mourn again
After that closing round
Mae rambles toward so faithfully
Is but a tinkling sound

Circling its vibrations through
Muddled, thin memory:
Lost Sam aloft earthward in air
Outplummeting Mae, me,

Beyond sad Leo's choky sobs
Making their ghostly breeze,
Filling the suds sailing around
Fair Aphrodite's knees.

A POSTHUMOUS EXHIBITION
OF THE ART OF ROBERT HUCK

Well, here we are, Bob.
Mountain, bird, bay, me . . . a gathering.
Black melancholy sun
Hanging beside a sea growth
In a rock. Light? Oh, light's
As glacial on the mountain,
On the falcon, on the ruins,
On the swan, as light can be.
It's in your tide pool—this one—where,
Uncoiling at the core,
It actually is growing
Now, is moving through the thing.
Earth people live to learn
About the deep. Dead center,
Bob, the seed that caught your eye,
Isn't it warm dead center?
Isn't that light inside?
The eagle and the hunters and the owl
Hang in the blizzard of our lives
With me, while there you are
All lit up, more at ease
Than when we talked of being
Here in heaven by the sea.

USHERS

"He had no desire to become an actor, any more than he had to become a musician. He felt no necessity to do any of these things; what he wanted was to see, to be in the atmosphere, float on the wave of it, to be carried out, blue league after league, away from everything."

Row after row, past shady little ponds
Of light, torn tinfoil glittering, our wands
Wagging the aisles (odor of bubble gum),
We led the eyes which longed for dreams to come
Into the holy Bryn Mawr Theater.
Behind the screen hunched Norway browns, their fur
Teased by the touching scent of spilled popcorn.
Our pace renouncing pimples yet unborn,
Treasuring dark, in livery, up and down,
With bony shoulders squared against our town,
We ushered housewives who could not stay home
About that vaguely Eastern pleasure dome
Of ice cream, candy, strange proximities:

Trembling hands astray near tragic knees,
The unwashed washed astride his nervous mare,
Cantering. O silver light! Flat thoroughfare!
None of us knew that some of us would gather
In time with alcoholics, Willa Cather,
Far from the talkies, in that silent, high,
Rose-ceilinged mosque of our Loop's other sky—
As quiet as the rats still crouched backstage—
Gaped at by film buffs glopping at old age,
To sit rereading our selves, face to face,
Conning our glow (which also was Paul's Case),
Libraried, winding up in Chicago—
O reeling light! O windy pigeons! Snow.

A SANDWICH FOR CELINA
BY A SPRING NEAR A REST STOP
IN CALIFORNIA

Like Hopkins' dream of tearful Margaret,
    poor squeaky little tad,
    muttering over weasel
    jaws washed down some
    twenty miles from Soda Creek
    from a well-guarded
    chicken ranch near Yreka,
    you're thinking now
    about your breezy fuzz,
    which flutters, and your
    doll, pup, pussy cat
    and fingernails—all so—
    for we do wonder why
    we moon about our eyes,
    in spare times (sometimes)
    make the best of bones
and beg the leaves to be rhetorical.

ABOARD THE OLD *NEW WALES*

In Memory of Richard Burton
(d. August 5, 1984)

Lord God, that's Lowry—Dylan in the nest
Crowing about this bottom of the sky.
No R.I.P., boys? Lyricals don't rest?
Well, not exactly my day. Tell you why.

Bloody dead soldier. August, '84,
Prophetic year for brilliant Eric Blair,
My anno alterations evermore—
Fifth vacant. Amen. Sunday's never fair.

I'd trade this shade to stage one live volcano
For dear cream's soulmate cupped under Milk Wood—
Where's Elpenor? Jack? Flynn? Napping below?
Workaday limbo this is and for good.

Millions of mournful echoes . . . listing ship . . .
Great-Gaffer-Charon grinning round his pole,
Full passage hot-palmed by that seaty grip,
All replay, ever, role by precious role.

Become Variety. Become Revue.
In from the cold aboard this musky ark,
My ghost treads on its selves here, two by two,
Down keylit gangways glowing through the dark

Of heaven's blackout blazing in the head.
Best parts merged in odd places out of time
(Chronology means nothing to the dead.),
All leads connected, everything in rhyme,

I rage bent boards in bards' immortal lights:
Petruchio, Kate's plume, topping the hay
As Philip Two's pride, juiced on glassy nights,
Defender of man's monumental clay,

Dreams of Darius on both scabby knees
Before crazed Alexandros' brazen kind—
Again key light each fresco, every frieze . . .
She-of-Illustrious-Parents couched in mind.

Dilly aloft embracing buxom clouds,
Down-the-Hatch-Jack stoking his matinee,
Backstroker-Malcolm sounding out cold shrouds—
O'Toole not yet. As my Becket would say:

We touch away the truth about God's task.
Ours to retongue every damned line we've learned—
Eternal lens . . . infinite ocean masque—
Ours to recall the planet-arts we earned.

Soon tearful Charley camping in the gin-
Clear need of love toward my pathetic pate:
"Bald as a tart's tit, Harry," reedy, thin
As my hold on Helen in that very late-

Night sleeper cribbed from rowdy Kit Marlowe:
"I'll fetch thee fire to dissolve it straight."
Lips fall apart and kiss again. The show
Boat *New Wales*, shoreless, rolls a Welshman's fate.

All mundane reels now cut beyond all mending,
Beyond myself in Technicolor frames,
I have become at last my acts unending
Within the play starcast with glossy names.

JUST LUCKY, I GUESS
For Sun, for You in Spring, Light Sleeper

> *"The head Byzantine or from*
> *Fayyum, the shoulders naked . . ."*

Your face, an easy gold, peaceful, serene
As Denise Levertov's vision of her husband
Carved fast asleep among his classic dreams,
Haloed in pillow cup and sun-bleached hair,
Rests here beside me, in the dawnlight asks:
What do *they* know about a one-night stand?
Tells several satyrs of lost, callous youth
To weep in place within my comic belly.

And eyelids tremble in the afterglow.

Although your names matter a lot to me,
Someone else knows which one it is, I hope.
The way you look right now, the little trees
A friend of mine says leaves hold in their branching
Are blue-green in those eyelids, claiming us
Dear as spring runs and long meanderings.
They touch me. Metaphor spells how we flow.
But you're already golden, love. Once more.

FOR A MAN WHO DIED QUICKLY ON A ROAD IN MEXICO

Instantaneous as dark
when the tube blows
in a motel's oddly
graceful instrument,
it is to be recalled
unlike forever—
as if the skittish house finch
on the apprehensive
perch of your remains
pecked at an everlasting
(in the first light on the highway)
nesty looking strand of hair
to start a cushion
for a traffic stopper.

CONCERNING POETRY

Think of yourself
in the aisle
of an airliner
mourning out loud
on the death
of a girl
none of them
happened to know—
arrival and deplaning
into Concourse D
handcuffed to luggage
unable to reach
the pen which
would unmake apologies.

ON THE MORNING OF THE DEATH OF ROBERT HILLYER

Robert Silliman Hillyer, from Pulitzer driven to post,
Finds in his smoky mirror a friendly looking ghost.

Draped in threadbare pinstripe (for things do come to pass),
His image whispers: Robbie, Lord knows all flesh is grass.

The maples near the meadow have run clean out of sap,
And God's down by the fence row taking a little nap.

This is the way it happens because the Spanish plains
Are mostly without moisture excepting when it rains.

The shadows of the poplars lean in their skinny shade
To punctuate the lyrical lines that aren't going to fade.

That amber light that's blinking is altering toward green.
And grateful Captain Nemo warms up the submarine.

TRIO: A FABLE

At one time I knew a woman who was so lovely about happiness that to look her over made your tongue too glad to sing. She had only one thing to do. She did not glitter when she walked. She glowed and shimmered like full moonlight on gentle water. Every part was of course: hips Aphrodite; hair Magdalen; lips Circe; eyes by night Diana, donkey-backed and holy-glazed by day.

The trouble was she had married a man who was sad about his timing. She met him on the road only because his living relatives had scared him into travel, for he was a listener and a watcher commonly subscribed to Wings, Sensations, Larks and Lucky Strikes in nearly that historical order. His dead folks smoke in lower Michigan. She called him bitter about noise, dumb, repetition, violence, hair, drugs, dogs, and dog shit caked on Cuban heels. He had not been happy or in style since he woke up one day in Peoria, Illinois, took a look, and remembered Whiting, Indiana, where he had once fallen for the daughter of an ex-chief petty officer who was also a cop. When Elvis charmed the taverns' T.V. audiences, he got worse because ear plugs didn't work, and he did have one hell of a cochlea problem deep in the inner ear.

This old-fashioned dream girl, who was determined to please, realized there was only one thing to do. She turned their home into it and called it Trio, because the times were bad (as her buck-eared husband knew), and she had to brighten up the skidding. Trio had three floors. When she got ready to keep on smiling, the ground floor was a child care nursery with a fenced-in yard. There was a parking lot, too, for motorcycles and compact cars without mufflers. The top floor was a whore house where the mothers of the children downstairs pleased the customers. Soon the most popular of these busy matrons was a girl named Regan Lear, who played cassettes of country music when she was on duty and who was so down home she kept a bottle of ketchup on her bedstand so that everything would taste folksy. The middle floor was a therapy center for the husbands of the women upstairs. This was all made possible by a federal grant pushed by a lobby sponsored by dentists who were investors in Japanese-made stereophonic equipment, motor bikes, and helmets with purple visors that made Jean Cocteau's early films look human.

During the tourist season Trio boasted a fairly swanky clientele including several graduates of Julliard who in their early 20's had got deprogrammed and were internationally famous rock singers. But the customers were mostly local boys. They came often and acted like flies that giggled. They wore funny hats, usually took off their high-heeled boots, and left wearing shit-eating grins commonly admired by teenagers and real-estate agents. And there is a moral to this quaint story. It is threefold: Happiness is love. Love is taking care of what is. The world must not be hateful.

After the moral, count on solitude. The crowded husband, who was in love of course, began to pine, to dwell upon his living relatives. But he could not afford his memory or his eyes—let alone those ears, so he walked out of town into a relatively quiet place near water. It was full of tules and green light, and he put his head down easy for a spell. A bittern woke him up, but the damned fool wasn't hungry. He saw wings, had sensations, realized three larks, and went sound asleep dreaming about love and Trio, which is today, although slightly altered, alive with smiles and busy.

APRIL 3, 1978

Fifty-four years now to the day
I uncurled like a fat cliché
Between wars, in their middle age,
My bottle-parents' bouncing rage,
Breathed in, stretched out, and took the shape
All organ grinders love: their ape.
Paid off then, proving pound for pound
How, also monkeying around,
God might have meant them to enjoy,
In miniature, in Illinois,
The apple and perhaps the core
Even in 1924.

Today my parents' middle years,
Noisy in fond jags, dreams, fits, tears,
Loud memories of first long pants
Uncomfortably alive with ants,
Appear tight-lipped each time I shave
Asking them what's to face, to save
For two girls and a bug-eyed son
Who count on killing getting done;
Who know their uncle slashed his wrists—
Something about which God exists,
Bombs, traps, the dull fix of bad times—
And that it's brutal if it rhymes.

LINES FOR WILLIAM GOLDING
1975

Sweet boys in groups of more
Than two are still the same.
They cruise the gentle shore
For any pretty game.

Even, at times, alone
A mean one of keen nose
Stands with a cocked hip bone
Between his struts to pose

Pictorial and grand
As David, while his small
Transistor in the sand
Declares him to be tall,

Like Adam, Elvis, man
Displayed on his own block,
Amplified by God's plan
To peddle roll and rock.

So be it so it goes
This sick year of small grace.
The blue flies buzz; the blows
In open wounds keep pace—

For how long who can tell?—
The great conch makes no sound
Above the metered yell
Whining, the beat, the pound.

Give me the lilting blues,
The leopard at my back,
Poplars lined up like peas,
The massive cardiac.

ONE SOBER MAY 18TH IN 1980

Rained on down here by aquamarine drizzle
Below the site of Malc and Margie's cabin,
Watching a documentary called "Volcano,"
I hear the shades of Wobblies hanged in Washington
Hack stringy ghosts into their spectral cups.
My gums bleed. Eerie Mount St. Helens grumbles.
My mind's wrong—*Incidentally, I smell* . . .
These dentures, like the Father of my Country's,
Must have been carved in the National Lab
Out of prime cherry felled in a petrified forest.
Their taste is bloody gin, my toast to Malcolm
Lowry, whose diminutive dong saved him
For us from being like his father, a wealthy
Guv who bought him off in time to give us
One big book we won't confuse with anything
Anonymous. For where we are, the poet says,
Is hell, and history, alas, tends to
Affirm the poet. Poor Lowry, born to praise
The likes of every bottle baby, who
In his time outdrank the local Dylans
And got his stone engraved: A one-shot man,
Counsels me from his leaky water wagon
As frame by frame the Celluloid unreels
An artful, clumsy man encircling
A boy revealed unbottomed on a bar
Stool in Oaxaca. Malc declares it is
A city of the dreadful night lit up.
Turtles flop in the sawdust beside two
Fawns gutted. Breath pure mescal, his voice now
Richard Burton's, Malc asks: "Would you believe
Their mother was butchered by a syphilitic?
In macho Oaxaca mild, sweet-assed bulls
Yearn to hump one another?" S.O.S.
He grins at an impaled buzzard puking

S.O.S., gapes at its mirror image—
S.O.S. Outside, the old volcano
Boils and burps. Baked ash falls on this tooloose
Lowrytrek around the weepy, circling man,
Rising in circles toward my own mean mouth.
Nobody moves now. Film flaps. It has ended.

KELLY SCANNELL ECHOES AT YELLOWSTONE

> *"Like from another time,*
> *that voice! Like sired by Caruso*
> *out of mustang Galli-Curci."*
> —Jim McQueen
> Cody, Wyoming

Those updraft arias that soared above
Ospreys the summer of our centennial,
Heaving up speech ghostlier than deep air
Once ranged beyond the genius of the sea
When I was maker of the song I sang,
Were my untrained sounds bouncing off those birds.
Park rangers with flamboyant, puckered hats
Plied me with vodka, failed, tried banishment,
Declared me one dried-out Tallulah Bankhead.
But when scouts from the Met arrived next year,
Contracts in hand, tuned ears euphorical,
Claiming my gift its proper audience—
Except for packrats and a zoo-born moose,
Three brown bears with inflamed interiors,
And something like the specter of Enrico
Haunting the cough of one outrageous cougar—
I became Yellowstone's oddball attraction,
Young faithful, pure vibrato, annual,
Inebriate of skinny oxygen.
I may sound off for Glacier or Grand Teton
Come our good Lord's year 1995.
These days, tourists, how sweet song prospers isn't
Any choice. My last time was a bummer
(I must have made a scared move way back when.
I failed to pluck my Amelita's splinter).
Whatever, I awoke corporeal
Within this poet who was pitiful, so
Minor we went hitch-hiking between seven

Academic sinecures and hauling coal
In Salt Lake when the main heat plant broke down.
That life approached placating hopelessness,
Worse than my warps occult and science fiction.
I never mooned baroque for opera,
But singers long to please their listeners.
Diva be damned, I'm happy with these ledges
Full of feathers, beaks, talons, scales, fins, bones,
Because the light is given. This time I
Cling to myself, cherish my part-time being
Banking Promethean these canyon walls,
Since what I sing is uttered word by word
Here in the air above the agile ospreys . . .
My owl-eyed belly rolling dream hair balls
To kill time for my new life's windy tongue.

WHILE THE NOW GENERATION BASKS IN ITS BRAND NEW MILKY WAY

For Tresa Hughes

My father mailed me fear.
My mother mooned on God.
The wafer in my mouth
Tasted a lot like sod.

Light failed so often then
I couldn't see to rhyme
Praise for a floating leaf,
Although I prayed for time.

Father cursed several bones
For bending at their knees.
Mother said: My dear son
To kneel is to say please

To him and to the wren,
Lily, and odd-ball auk,
The sea anemone—
Grace too the low marsh hawk—

Afterward that sweet mare
Gaited on ruddy coals
Who shied around the field's
Damnable gopher holes.

And suddenly the girl
Who was to be my wife.
We kissed. She fled away
Giving us back our life

Divided such as those
Who listen, look, and find
Heart's flesh is manifold:
Cannot and can be kind.

HALLELUJAH
Converted by the Good Books of the '60s

I wake up thinking Bruce J. Friedman's mother
Is nagging me for having drunk too much.
She's right. I fell asleep with Malamud's
New book at page three nestled in my beard.
So I get up and move like Poldy Bloom
In minor ecstasy quick for the john—
Portnoy-erotic about privacy.
Lucky at love, I look out at the Bay
Of Bellingham, the soft San Juans, also
Erotic, surely, about clouds. Jollies
Lean toward the harbor and, of course, the gulls
Are Jews, the bluebills and the spirit ducks
Like little blessings patterned for the yawls.

I think I'd feel as Isaac Babel did
Mounting up with the Cossack cavalry,
But clip-clop jades are gone . . . like Maxwell Street . . .
Bellow's old Loop, Algren's ticked-off South Side . . .
Me among Texans with the toggle switch
Warm in the high sun heading for Cologne,
Kid gentile angel shot out of the blue . . .

For almost one now, weird and orderly
As Delmore Schwartz sleep-walking through daydreams,
My mind's clearly elated with the small
World at my window, Singer's chosen view,
From which not even pigeons fly like goys—
So good-bye, Lindy, and perhaps hello
To Him whose rainbow will seems to have turned
Or who remembers better since He died.

CARRIED AWAY

Ms. Binnie Bohn, whose eyes glowed like dark honey,
Tucking me in her pocket for a spell,
Said: Love your angle, sweetheart, more than money,
And underneath this clover isn't hell.

Be still, she sighed, a stroll will do you wonders.
You've ranted on how much you like it here.
When lightning cracks and you catch little thunders,
Vibrations common to my hips, don't fear

Those dream-squalls you can handle in my pocket
While we continue barefoot through this park,
Our meadow, now as friendly as a locket
Inside which photo portraits face the dark.

Ms. B.'s deep marrow strayed across the meadow,
Swayed by the motion of her leafy walk,
Leading us through translucence toward the shadow
Which spelled her glow and made the tree frogs gawk.

WATCHING HEARTTHROBS ENGAGE THE STRAIT OF GEORGIA

For Anthony Hecht

Watching heartthrobs engage the Strait of Georgia,
I think of Priam keening to Troy's wall.
Achilles lords the day, his prize yet mortal.
We're still beside ourselves—If I recall

When, nearly vast as Ingres' Turkish Women
(Transported East, far east of Chicago),
The bolder girls in the Medina Tower
Basked in the ultraviolet overglow;

My father racked down State St. with his nobles;
Mother kept household, gin and bitters cold;
And I played brave for keeps with my best marbles
Because we never lost then, I was told . . .

Except as mock-Huns crouched between Alhambra
And the Granada Arms across the street
Scouting the vacant pee-wee golf course rubble
For fresh-killed Belgians Boche were out to eat;

How once, heart-struck by calf-eyed Helen Twelvetrees,
My teacher, and a classmate's sister's friend,
I wept to think that Rudolph Valentino
Alone was Allah's favored in the end;

When, between wars, father's Shrine-plume bobbed homeward,
Maneuvering staircase, floating through the hall,
Mistook my room for love's twice, and, like Hector's,
Nodded above the face that could not fall—

We're now beside our has-beens here, old trooper.
The grand Medina Tower gleams no more.
This pair hugs in a tide through which are gliding
Snorkeled, grey-prowed computers just off shore.

Our planet-watching world, electric, touchy
About its place, its space, curtain and wall,
Holds chances are no I.D. card's a winner
And, heads or tails, each toss is timed to fall.

Drink to the moon then, sun, the Strait of Georgia;
To Homer, friend; reft Priam full of tears;
To Ingres, always more than fair with Helens;
These sweethearts wading into airborne years.

THE HEARING

To the Attorney General of
the Province of British Columbia
     Garde Gardom

This spanking brand new assistant D. A.
could operate that dark suit (by Du Pont)
without a hand too long in either pocket,
something it must have taken months to learn
working it downright hard. To keep his cool
(His first love flame? God? Maybe Cotton Mather)
he'd rigged a face like an expensive condom
with fixed eye-skin you don't expect will tear,
so that it shocked hell out of both of us—
after the mouthpart burst, before he got
that damned suit out of high—to hear him shout:
"I mean you, yes, you, sir, and Mary Wanna!"
while fresh-boiled hide broke forth all by itself.

BACK YARD PATROLLED BY BLUE JAYS IN THE BARE YEAR 1980
(A Fable for Eugène Ionesco)

*"The poet is a bird who must
sing in his genealogical tree."*
—Jean Cocteau

Let's have it with the warbler over there,
That fat one pecking at the call bird's willow,
Whose chubby feathers scheme up lukewarm water
Lapping her backside in his dream birdbath,
Who pecks at love, longing to think about it
Until down curls close to his memory—
Praise Elvis, does this one look viable?
What he's learned about water's for prime drakes
Slipping between the tules artfully
As yeasty seeds timed to lilt on the tongue.
He chimes off-key. Let's bump his baleful liver
Until it bongs and bells a tolled moonrise
To show this loony who's allowed to pout.
If bats don't flap around Mick J. St. Rollo
So that the blood bleats for its boiling bones,
We'll know our busted thrush cocked for the cooler's
Not the dissenter we were looking for.
Meantime, he's acting edgy. Let's not banter.
His water-dripping tone's too amorous.
Let's cram that bawdy fluting down his throat
Before he charms a hasty murmuration.
Toss this hemp up—Such tunes are perilous.
We'll teach his toes to twitch demotic time.
A sound tie on that alder and he'll dangle
Neatly, look just historical as hell
To those nostalgic, blue-capped, nervous cacklers
Whose naughty twits mourn for his throttled neb.

HOT DIRGE FROM A FLOP

In Memory of Ethel Merman

I'd like to hear God has a Greenpeace plan
For plants and animals and even man.
I'd like to know George Orwell was a char-la-tan,
But this year I don't think I can.

Some time ago the word got out that should
Tibetan lamas move to Hollywood
Mount Everest would not comment on who fled,
Fled, fled!
Everyone knows that Mr. Kurtz is dead.

Each morning I get up to find the sun
That sizzled for both Shakespeare and John Donne
Is ired by a sky that looks like lead,
Lead, lead!
Yes, Housman tuned in on what Hardy said.

I love your being, honey, bounce and bone,
But nonetheless I'm going to live alone.
I couldn't bear to share with you this dread,
Dread, dread!
Oscar knew why love tries but kills instead.

The dark pulse pumps no wagging tail, alas,
And light dim-little seldom comes to pass.
My point is Job's big book by far was red,
Red, red!
Count Leo knew, and later Conrad said—
No matter, lover, which boat or which bed—
The river flows, but Mistah Kurtz—he dead!

ROCK MUSIC SARA MADE ME IN BERMUDA

Some guys say they don't know
Why love is come and go
Because they haven't figured out their traumas.

Trouble with that damned thang
Sweet cowpokes call poontang
It Oedipulls you backwise to your mamas.

Which happens when it starts
Creeping up on your hearts—
Shanghais you, trips you off to seek Grand Lamas

In Chi-town and New York—
Flying the same old stork—
St. Louis, New Orleans, the soft Bahamas,

Till, wrinkles linked by change,
In time this gets less strange
(Lucky or not, we launder our small dramas.)

Because that bold, sad thang
Bouncing its wing and wang
Pops poontang home. Lord bless our round, warm mamas.

KEMO SABE

At Argentcare in Ithaca, New York,
Spartikos Pappas Winds His Beads to Sleep
A Legend for Leslie Fiedler

Bright .45's at hand each randy night,
His powder dry, pulse sounding every bead,
One silver keepsake bullet saved to bite,

He dreams of Tonto, kin, dim nursery light
In which he mounts a miniature steed,
Toy .45's at hand each dandy night.

Bedazzled by masked boys, his uncle, bright
Old blade, intones Rossini's Ranger's Creed:
Hi-Yo, Silver! My bullet's grace to bite!

Spartie, his doting mother's brave delight,
Carrier of his father's stoic seed,
Bright .45's at hand one randy night,

Jay Silverheels, bronze, gallops into sight.
Theirs grows into dear love, declines to need
The silver keepsake bullet saved to bite,

Until Jay, bareback, and his star-eyed knight
Are godforsaken, bushwhacked here to bleed.
Bright .45's at hand each randy night,
One silver keepsake bullet saved, they bite.

CENTERFOLD COPY
FOR THE GIRL NEXT DOOR

His heeled-high Stetson howl-brimmed loud yahoo,
My pa's nicknamed Prosperous Merryway;
Penned our bad karma up with porcupines;
Subscribes to *U.S. Folk-Twang Plum Review*;
Sells Nashville high in Philadelphia.
My guy's moustache dangles right prime Zapata.
I'm pretty-two dream pounds plump Cherokee,
Twelve centimeters Ute. My private parts,
Pinched Cantonese slipped between peace-pipe Sioux,

Feel seat-belt-neat's-foot coy in my tight Honda.
Ma tutored my moonlit diminutives
Till fit to throb, downed twisty metrical,
They mingled with the sun and glowed in cozy.
She reckoned diet shaped such lights true blue.
Broiled killdeer cold-cocked three puts before noon
Waxes my hipsway this side of abnormal.
Some call me Amber. I love Jacques Cousteau,
Dolphins—cocaine, dig?—borzois and rock Bizet.

ASSAY IN RHYME
Cold Comfort from Professor Emeritus Kindel

A fool might once himself alone expose;
Now one in verse makes many more in prose.

Disinterested in sex, faith, color, race,
Let's both admit this is a testing place.
Regardless who's confronted by which faction,
Most people find pure joy mounts with firm action.
First, how do you react to seminars
Where credits feature critics in star wars?
Fine. Truth starts with a grim, straight-forward question.
What with meek peers, doggerel, indigestion,
Don't you feel letdown sometimes, slightly leery?
Good. What you need is fragile Blossom Dearie.
This isn't Oxford. You're not nearly barmy.
Her discs turn up at the Salvation Army,
Where also on occasion you'll find boots
Toed as nostalgic as moth-eaten suits.
Don't mix your megrims up with widow's weeds.
Wise second-story men wear well-worn tweeds—
Which is my main point; Cultivate the wary,
Forget the source. Covet the secondary.
My stewardship succeeds here like these rhymes,
Golf, bridge, my wife—a living March of Dimes—
Reminds me, if you choose to share your sack,
Settle for pale, severe, in grey or black.
Save fox-heads for your secret, private habits.
You're not alone. This can is packed with Babbitts.
Dorothy Thompson was no college try.
She drank with Lewis, Sinclair, not North Frye.
Don't think this hedged flop hit ground terrified
Because God's pulse was partial to your hide.
Mystics don't read, aren't forward, never vicious;
They're absolutely, simply superstitious;

Don't dig beach parties; get unlikely fun
By bending down grasswise beamed on the sun.
Wild hares, however, whose translucent ears
Twitched in their Eden, magnified man's fears.
Although our eyes outgrow the Sunday funnies,
They touch us still, blink, hanker after bunnies,
And make some men damn rich—as you well know—
In Copenhagen, Stockholm, Chicago.
A hamstrung man crippled by rants and rails
Can Easter near a clutch of cottontails.
Mine was a brainy girl whose amber belly
Bounced perfect (wore her hair like Mary Shelley).
Her mimicry set my young heart aglow:
"Soccer good to me; baseball I-doe-know."
She liked her gin. I doted on her fur.
We hugged a lot and felt warm where we were.
Think on this when your whistle's out of tune:
A break's assured every too-late-warm June.
Haul ass to Scotland, swill, hold down your haggis.
Grab a jet skyhound tourist to Las Vegas.
Invent. Imagine fame purrs at your hips.
Try on Mick Jagger; yours are ample lips.
When that gets itchy, scratch. If you get antsy,
Forget Coleridge and cuddle up with fancy.
Rub down an edgy filly. Have a ball.
Pay up. Hang tight. Hope autumn holds off fall.
Be at once palpable and in a trance
And thereby cherish twice one remembrance.
Beat blackjack, roll, win, ramble, wing it proud—
Bland schoolmarms get reborn lost in a crowd.
But keep in mind your salary. Getting laid
Depends on reappearing here afraid.
Don't gossip about everything I say.
Gobble the gist. Order PMLA.
The son of odd old Vita Sackville-West
Knew how to back off treading at his best,

Controlled himself, bloomed on his buried betters
By editing Virginia Woolf's posh letters.
Dwelling on Don Quixote's flaky lights,
Recall Cervantes' last, crazed, hungry nights.
Don't moon about lifting a battered shield
For anyone the likes of Kate Mansfield,
Nèe Beauchamp, Kathleen, strangely in a flurry
To vanish before John Middleton Murry.
Feodor's wife pinched pennies, feared he'd leave her
For one good card (Let's not speak of John Cheever;
The cramped colon, that painful lower bowel
That grappled with the tripe for Robert Lowell.).
Forget T. B., Mann's *Mountain*, Lowry's torments,
Neglectful Frieda, fits, death, D. H. Lawrence,
John Keats, without tuberculin's last fix,
Hacking his lost lungs up at twenty-six.
A campus is a lark, a Gerber titty,
A magic molehill sandbox kind of city.
If you've decided that you're here to stay,
Shut up. I've got the duller left to say.
When you teach of course a history of films,
Don't focus on those classic keels and helms
That got mixed up with kinky girls and gin
Far off the pirate set with Errol Flynn.
Never face your cards up on the table.
Praise Eisenstein. Be snide about Clark Gable.
Don't let your wrist hang limp near Noel Coward.
Rely on neat roles swelled by Leslie Howard,
Whose eyes convinced us he—not Scarlet—sinned,
Sold out, and left us all *Gone with the Wind*.
Senator Bankhead's daughter learned to row
In *Lifeboat*, but depend on Jean Cocteau
To grab your students deep down in their vitals.
Converge on foreign films with English titles.
Stick to this text: Praise. Criticize. Don't say
One word about Cocteau and Jean Marais.

Private lives speak for suicidal bards.
Save your days off to wisecrack your petards
And then hedge every casual comment
Against our new charge: sexual harassment.
Yours may well be the age of rock and roll,
But God pits every cherry in each bowl.
Whatever years of reading sometimes bring
Be doubtful of a notion that takes wing.
Beware of bars, beer barrels, wit, warm chatter,
Blank paper, ink, and, Lord knows, subject matter.
Waves are not made without a little storm.
When you're neck-deep nibble on rules and form.
For instance, caged lyrics may sound precise,
But summing up, one's lines must breed like lice
Contained within a seamless goatskin sack
Tongue-stitched in Wales to tease Jack Kerouac.
Observing soaring ospreys, dives, wet fetchings,
Imagine rubbing London birds, old etchings.
They say, although he'd kneel before a rose,
Simple St. Dunstan pinched the devil's nose.
Opposites. I spent prime years poking fun
At male orangutans and became one—
Beats Garbo downtown maybe, skin and bone.
My tree's banana wants to be alone.
When offspring gather close to shadow me,
I fade into my branchy pedigree,
Where I can tell right good wings hardly thrive
Yet keep hawk claws aloft and help bees hive.
Ambivalence clings to man's point of view.
My nature has confused me. Has yours you?
The market like the sun falls low and rises.
Teacher, this life's chock-full of sweet surprises.
In '86 Pemberton patented Coke;
Died broke in '87, friend, no joke.
Seaside on summer sand for sunlight's sake
The young stretch (topless) out to bake a cake

Which they can't call their own and chomp on too.
Lord knows, dear lad, there's one cold law that's true:
Proximity of time and any place
Is the wax ball we're rolled in face to face.
Now hear this very clearly and take note.
In '79, sailing a ten foot boat,
A Minnesotan, name of Gerry Spiess,
Bobbed off to seek his long-tailed Golden Fleece.
This manic fellow with Midwestern motion
Successfully crossed the Atlantic Ocean.
He wasn't a wing nut. He wasn't insane.
He spent that trip unlonesome, read Mark Twain.
Might say he carried his pilot to sea—
If you're that risky, Christ, don't count on me.
Caution's my byword. Move slow with the times.
Avoid most bells and anything that chimes.
Never forget your early childhood fear;
Those little echoes in your inner ear
Thrive on the pages you are left to teach
About, around, but not bullseye. Don't preach.
Be calm, polite, prim, shifty, do your part
As do all honest men who distrust art.
Your voice, anonymous, won't haunt your grave
The rest is frail. In this game what's to save
Is real estate and damned good, hard, cold cash
Earned without hacking literary trash.
Otherwise prayerful bywords here: "Survive—
Lord, may I thole after I'm sixty-five."
Time polishes the sycophantic guile
That pleases deans and pampers punk lifestyle.
Chest felled and bagged, the aching scrotum sagging,
School bell a-clang, and your doomed tongue still wagging,
Wiping your anus with harsh public tissue,
Address yourself likewise to every issue.
Speak to the pitchfork's feel for common fodder
In *Scitan Buleskeid* (Robert's Rules of Order).

Manure does heap a meager pile of fun
Over the old saw's essence: "It's all one."
Committees don't need reasons. When *they* rhyme
They mean we like to gather wasting time
Bitching at cut-backs, fidgeting our bums,
Fiddling anew with old curriculums.
Hip to what cups fad's ear and bathes its eye,
We star Bob Dylan's lyrics, list sci-fi
(Of course when low enrollment's really biting
Our standby sweetsop's still creative writing.).
Pass by majority this votive adage:
"May fashion ever grace the Noble Savage."
Rocked in God's lasered, starry vast, we beep
Time's odd beam back and swing our branch to sleep.
It took us eons to brave down the trees,
Ages to stage our grandstand off our knees.
So help me, son, history lags, balks, lingers—
Hard to believe how we uncurled our fingers
(Blind brutes spellbound in motion for the sake
Of change, meat, or some dim spinal mistake) . . .
Courted the moon with Sidney, outsoared air . . .
Brought lunar rocks to folks who worship hair,
Idolize Elvis' ghost, was on sit-coms,
Fondle brown petals bedside after proms,
Wake to the steady musical alarm
That rings each being in its body's charm,
Where Levi's lay commends the crooning bun
To oglers that our species' will be done.
When Lawrence poked the great grey merger, Walt,
He pegged our Pygmy yen for bawdy salt
Where god-balled bulls once swayed through buttercups.
It's landings, take-offs, lad, sky-blue hang-ups.
In college towns you plan for pleasant kids
Who deal in dope but never hit the skis,
Get Hallmark tearful over whales, stray puppies,
Low grades, who yearn to grow up into Yuppies,

Process wild oats, subscribe to Henry Luce
(Pity that silly old prof on the juice!).
They're sure Dad's bread is theirs in several banks,
Even daydream sometimes of saying thanks,
Guess now they're cramming to be So-and-So
Because Mom dated No-Place-Else-to-Go.
Some will be sent away to better schools
Where they may learn a humane set of rules,
Reject the law: Birth, copulation, death—
Let us both pray, while there's polluted breath,
That, loathing syntax, dreading precise diction,
They'll realize Orwell ain't science fiction;
That one at least or maybe, perhaps, two
Will get this joke I've played on me for you
In hot air from a weary muscle sack
And heave off quick, cut, leaving us the slack.

A FETISH FOR MOLLY

Occasionally as the sound of spring,
Something transports so cautiously my bones
I kneel before the plumbing you've been near—
Odd marrow, I suppose, or then perhaps
The sweet smell death demands of your live parts
Reminds me why I used to genuflect.
Being involved with everything you do,
I'd pray to marigolds this morning, girl,
If my pulse now weren't counting on my heart
Because you've turned these elbows bountiful.

AT THE MIRROR ON NEW YEAR'S DAY

As Doc says now continually
I rearrange the order of Yeats' trip
to Byzantium. Emotionally,
that is, we're realized; I yearn,
you eat, get hungrier. We need
with passion half-assed animal
all women, several loonies, light,
my wife, and, on occasion, the small
translucence of a backward frog.
In other words, our problem's in my head.

Take moving toward you in this frame
of mind tells me in Doc's voice almost:
"Wish him well." Poor thing, if I were
easier, friendlier with your being
natural, I would believe my ears.
Even your eyes might be acceptable . . .
feeling up windy, sunlit hair,
raping a pair of migratory bones,
making our move together so to speak
in time prescribed for gross reflections.

HISTORICAL MAY DAY, 1968

All by myself in the periodical room,
I look out the open library window
To see my students milling around the fountain.
It's brand new and therefore a holy thing.
A few are swimming in the round, green pool
But most are staring at the three-story column,
A solid white jet onto whose peak, bobbing gently,
Is moored, they say, a perfect replica
Of the Graf Zeppelin, which cannot blow,
I hear one sophomore cry, because H. Rapp Brown,
At ease at the controls, has issued the right orders.
This therapeutic vision of bright girls, boys, water,
Is doing fine when suddenly a whip cracks . . .
Clatter, sound of twin, loud axles, harness squeak,
Boom of big barrels breaking—In the square (what else?)
Appears the Old Guard at full gallop: Budweiser's
Belgian Per herons, fetlocks feathered, stallion-eyed
That noisy, monumental team reins in
For water, with free beer, and right below
The dirigible, which revs up, rises slowly
With its belly, even slower, opening,
And on which there are turrets now, I hear.

THE CROSSING: A SHORT STORY

When Ponce Greenstein found himself really hauling
His wheezes up the Wilson Avenue
El's mean stairs, he thought about bold dramas
He had cherished in a crowd. He recalled
The sizzling man, philosophized about
A third-rail barbecue versus a gun shot
With most commuters struck dumb-talkative
And one or two pried tipsy off brass rails,
Their glazed eyes true containers of a world
That moved, God knows, nearby, emotional.
"Pawn," as his good friends teased him, had small thoughts
Which often turned into such grand occasions
That briny pickle barrels got figurative
Enough to smell, yes, metaphorical:
Cucumbers, folksy, following themselves
Around a bumpy whirlpool, circling,
Within their steel-bound wooden universe.

That sounded good to Pawn when he arrived
At last in breathless agony to stand
Among his kind atop the cold platform,
Wondering if these railways in Chicago
Might carry one to stops above strange parks
With little streams cutting through manicured
Fairways that twinkled when the moon was out—
Queer star-bear, sky fish, hunter, distant cove
Tricking the lunar, tidy side of love.
Thus dreamy, Pawn boarded the north-bound el.

Across the aisle a hairy, young adult
With eyes like rhinestones clutched a guitar case.
Hooked on the head beside his were what looked
To Pawn like ear parts of a stethoscope
Leading into a compact stereo.

Eye's partner's fingernails, chomped to the quick,
Were lacquered blue. Dangling from each tooled belt
The leather pouch sacred to brotherhood
Beyond Adidas' emblems on their shirts,
Their Stetson replicas and cowpoke boots—
Beyond Pawn, too, who dozing off conjured
Up Tommy guns, felt hats, violin cases,
Dillinger, Cagney, Scar Face Al Capone,
Bogart, George Raft, Edward G. Robinson—
Slept like the dead, awoke in Evanston,
And got off quickly at an unknown stop
Feeling somehow he had planned arriving at
A station where he'd find himself alone.
History wasn't holy, but this place
Recalled a spark barely alive in him,
A tiny, far speck beckoning him back
To boyhood: "Dare you, Greenstein! Doubledare!"

Pawn jumped up. God, without a drink in years,
He thought he had D.T.'s. That gradeschool whine,
The bully's nasal twang: "Dare you, Greenstein!"
Still echoed too damned clearly. Why recall
A scrawny, pimply bastard's doubledare?
Yet Pawn, dead earnest now on getting home,
Walked to the platform's edge and looking down
Studied the tracks, lining up each third rail,
Then eased his toes onto the splintered ties
(Touch of young Ponce, wheeled mid war-amputees
Whose caged stumps hailed the Loop's parading ladies).
Surprised, he crossed, reaching the south-bound side
Unharmed, alive, grasping the platform boards
And managing—behold—to chin himself
And swing his aching gut to safety, where
His vision of the sizzling man, too vivid
In the inner eye, dropped, and he vomited
Neatly, chin off the platform's edge, to mark

The manic finish of his marathon.

Leaving the Bryn Mawr station, Ponce Greenstein
Grinned like a true Scout trooped beyond the Den.
In truth Pawn knew recaptured youth, briefer
Than birthdays, fell away and turned upon
The dreamer in his mirror heartless images
As well-defined as cruel photographs.
He thought about the friends who nicknamed him—
Many of whom these days kept to their rooms—
Crossed Kenmore and, determined to forgive
All bullies past, present, living or ghosts,
Pawn stopped at Goldberg's for corned beef, a dill,
A quart of milk to go, arriving home
Worn out to find he'd left the innerdoor
Down, unmade, clogging half the living room,
A sloppy symbol of his time's demands,
Or meager blessing maybe. What the hell,
Pawn grumbled, a surprising night today.
So now a salty trickle. So fatigue.
Tears on rye crusts, the stem-end of a pickle—
Small rent, let's hope, to pay one plucky guy
Whose feet decided being in my shoes
Compulsive why not foolishly yet brave
The child-dark of a wrinkled boy's bad dream.

MARGARET AS A STILL LIFESAVER

Once in nine-
teen sixty
bet your life
my lap dog's
eye focused
this framing
then ready
so that the
held light's still
upon one
dimpled girl
shadowed by
a mountain
looking at
the surface
of a lake
because she
was flat out
that much that
day in love
with floating.

WILL ROGERS SAYS TO WILEY POST*

Having no Latin, friend, and with all due
consideration for the real fact that
according to Ripley Roger Ascham
actually wrote so hard attempting to
commemorate the tenth anniversary
of his Queen's coronation that he died,
I reckon that shore bird off our port wing
wouldn't be much help right now if he could
tell us about the cold on either side.

On August 15, 1935, Will Rogers and his friend Wiley Post died when Post's plane crashed fifteen miles from Point Barrow, Alaska.

GIRL OF THEIR DREAMS
How Libby Seized the Day in Fayetteville

*The novel has had its day, we are
assured, and in the Age of Aquarius,
film, man, film's the stuff that will
do more than fiction can to justify
God's way to man.*
—Mordecai Richler

*In headaches and in worry
   Vaguely life leaks away,
And Time will have his fancy
   To-morrow or to-day.*
—W. H. Auden

Lover, beloved, sit graveside
On the grass in Arkansas.
He feels like well-aged mutton
Clasped in a polished claw.

How goes the past? she questions.
Does your mind, like cold cream,
Flunk childhood in Chicago
Or does it help to dream

About the dead all summer
Down here where mocking birds
Manage a sound more pleasing
Than art, in your own words?

She asks: Old has-been usher,
How did you like the smell
Looped in the *Oriental* with
Sinatra's show and tell?

Didn't, he says. Paul Muni,
Magical Orson Welles,
And Seattle's Frances Farmer
Put clappers in my bells.

Sweetmeat, you guys are crazy—
Deadbeats, cold, sweaty snores—
The way you soaped those saddles,
Went riding off to wars,

Makes me believe there's something
Between you and my clit
More blank than space, mad Patton's ace.
Maybe our heads don't fit.

Perhaps this world has changed so
Much *we* might as well be
Planted below with Paul and Fran
For all that I can see.

He says: Hon, if life's twisty,
It's got something to do
With grass and cemeteries, sun-
Light this way, me . . . you,

The turn your hand keeps taking
For more than what was prime
When I got back from overseas
To find out just in time

That you were in the offing.
Practical as that pig
Who kept the wolf beyond the door.
You didn't give a fig

If dream girl's films got burned up,
Her wild-west town once prized
Turned out to be Detroit with wings,
Frances lobotomized . . .

But Libby's eyes find shadows.
She stands: you poor, sad ghost!
Here's the right place for you to shake
The soot off our Gold Coast

And clutch your grab-bent clapper
And clang your rusty bell.
Don't shed a tear for me, my dear.
Scamper backward toward hell—

Fig? Press that leaf in *Playboy*.
I'm not your guilty pig.
Remember Frances Farmer was
My kind of girl first. Dig?

IN MEMORY OF WILFRED OWEN
November 11, 1984

Plain poetry, an antique itch . . .
Today good soldier in a ditch—
His odd sound, that is, as he starts
To realize his world departs
For no dark down or blue above
But drifts far off away from love—
Mumbles, perhaps, god yes, aloud
About the moon behind a cloud
(For we do whisper to the sky
After our earthward's getting high)—
Tells, tongue in cheek, great oaks and pines
Acorns and needles share their lines.

It's how we talk when we're pure dumb
In praise of light on pear and plum
Or when a nervous wound takes wing
Airing those bones which want to sing.
Right now, say, how I wish to feel
(Far from the trigger and warm steel)
About that soldier in my head
Who murmurs he's not really dead,
Just joking, kind of on the lam,
Scared, AWOLED, acting like a ham,
Being himself still, taking care
To grin at those guys over there.

WITH ALBERT PINKHAM RYDER
ON A BAY IN PUGET SOUND

It is almost too charming for the eye,
Fetched wings more common than Bell's sagging lines,
Shingles that glitter as Cézanne revealed,
Finches, the swallow evening as first stars
(Already happy?) seem to know about
The sunlit bugs' small sleep. So this postcard
Is Ryder's, while the sea itself, whitecapped,
Becomes the tight bird's bobber when the moon
Returns to put her on display, the wet
Curve throbbing and the silver hair. She lifts
Shell, shrimp, sways coral, says: Now. Here. Look here.
Green, foolish blue man, look who's beckoning.

PASSING THROUGH

My patched fact in this alley
being gentle with the cans
knows every hungry town roach
hugs it passion—

doesn't fear wear now,
nag my nagging action,
move little movers carelessly.
Otherwise age involved,

merchants will never miss me,
labor's not my faction—
Voters, may godkind keep you
for the while.

ROSE OF HIS WORLD

Fresno: in front of someone's stucco house
while second wife with whose first daughter slept,
he stood akimbo on the sandbur lawn;
the best well-oiled Armenian long gone,
full moon his own becoming ping-pong ball,
swaying, he might almost have caught himself—
when there he was, confronted by a rose.
One blossom, also swaying, on the one
bush in the sandburs stopped someone.
Moonlit the bucket and his needled feet,
moonlit the water carried to the bush—
Moonlit whose house? part of which woman's knee?
child's finger? and a corner of what face?
were someone's lost because the rose was where
nothing else but that man, who also swayed,
was, at that time, in California.

A GENTLE WARNING
TO GOD'S BRAVE SWAN WILLOW

He was the kind who bought a green Jaguar
To cart his eyes around in every evening,
A country sailor who knew why the hills
Modeled his sky. That ship purred heavenly.
Ridges approached blue lakes. Mermaids got leggy.
Time, proximity, fads, dark fears, and love
Slipped in a viscous hug around hot pistons.
All green-capped slopes were artfully freewheeling.
She waited in a valley, hopeful fair.
She waved until their touch undressed them quickly.
Later they called you Swan because her name
Was Willow. Yes, heart's mouth, incredible,
Brings the warm body to its brainy tongue.
Cramped hands, prehensile, open like a sigh.
New love licks down. Beauty is treacherous.
Twilight upon it is an amber kiss
Shaping the eyes. Hitchhiking's garrulous.

THE PACT

In the tent on
Robert Creeley's
lawn is really
close to aging
neatly in clean
skins fresh from the
Frigidaire, yet
on occasion,
because there are
women in there,
the window is
opened and we
are invited
to be ourselves
even before
sea and mountain
but never al-
lowed to make war.

CLAIR DE LUNE

My great grand-père, Amadie Jardin . . . beloved,
I'm told, for saying, "Good. It's good, all good . . ."
The sweet man's sperm conceived its Hollywood lean-to
Nearby Lake Champlain with a moonlit Mohawk girl
Who mumbled: "Madie, oh, you knew we would,"
In patois with a pair of puffy lips,
Unminding heart, no oil of citronella
(Touching can talk us out of suicide).
Saturday nights she feasted on fat clouds,
Envisioning her wondrous appetite.
On Sundays they marched arm in arm to Mass.
Don't bug me. Mid-week scratched around their itch.
I can't begin to know their daylight clover,
The salty bees, mosquitoes, and the humming
Of the horseflies, or her filmy lunar hips.
I dream about moonbeam, sea, river, lake,
Vast marshes, wet knolls, God knows, silver water,
Beads of humidity, squirm, give and take.
Grand-mère declared the old man praised the lap
His head recalled closer than copper mines,
T. B., good wine, rockers, or even palsy.
My puzzle's how her daughter weathered this:
A night nurse drawn to silent matinees,
Whose sleepy eyes longed for their private naps.

MUNICIPAL PARK

Sit-napping on a splintered bench where loss,
Regret, at heart forgotten sorrow,
Twisty as ivy, are trying
To remember how he used to
Think he liked to feel, he tosses bread crumbs
To lousy, red-eyed pigeons, who,
Wobbly as old guys anyway,
Get him to feed the while on how
Years rolled him toward this hatred of the wheel.

FOUND BOTTLED IN A TIDE POOL NEAR LINCOLN CITY, OREGON, ADDRESSED TO M. S. B.

Solo these days reminds me Captain Nemo
Was a favorite of a lonely friend of mine
Who told me that bassoons once had three keys
For which Vivaldi composed skillfully.
He claimed this woodwind moved him through vast swells
On highs and lows whose undertows' haul tugged
Him into dipsomania until
He longed to drink small seas of Tanqueray.
So true to us, he said, the double-reeded.
Floating the border side of Boundary Bay,
My memory of the sound of a bassoon
Recalls your voice saying this instrument,
Cherished by Papa Haydn, was refined
And boasts today twenty-two keys to liquefy
Its range. Ah, love, you are expansive too,
Verily moon-pitched, tonic, deep they say.
That friend of mine in waves not unlike Nemo's
Did reel himself astray. A castaway
Myself, drifting without you, I'm not so low
I can't cork up good news. George Zukerman,
Our world's premier bassoonist, is alive
Ashore and thriving in White Rock, B. C.—
Which reminds me that I'd give both right ventricle
And left testicle if you'd happen to
Find yourself, solo, northward bound for lessons.

POSTSCRIPT

I mean after
nightcrawlers like
moonlit pythons,
loud poplar leaves,
orioles, pike,
geraniums,
picnics, wrens, girls,
beer, yellow gin—
your late rainbows—
when it becomes
difficult to
choose between a
block meerschaum and,
say, getting laid,
you pretty damn
well ought to be
squeamish about
Edward Albee.

BOY IN THE SUBURBS

In Memory of Ben Shahn

Stumbles in high out of the house
against his father's car . . . fenders,
a sloping trunk inside of which
keep still some keepsakes of the family . . .
tentative reach for fin to pull
himself upon that slope and flip
onto his back. What does he intend?
He cannot truly love that goddam Ford,
but slow slide downward, then the grab
at chrome strip and the upward tug again,
ease, the beginning downward, then
the haul back, easier, another glide.
This takes place seven times before he smiles
the mounting of his bicycle, grinning
right arm toward heaven, every knuckle
in control, rides off, legs churning
through the neighborhood—Oh, this
child's made to make do anywhere.

MACKENZIE BRIDGE

Light in the needles, undulating flights,
The Hawthorne blooming, rose and whites. Last night
A backcast, perfect, hovering, retrieved
A small bat, jaws clamped on a worn bucktail.
Believe me, that queer mouse and Dracula
Didn't have much in common. Air is air.
The swallows, little more than what they mean,
Do as I would hereafter . . . Or to wake
In the restored well house in Bloomington
With Hoagy's "Stardust" carved into the wall,
Dead drunk again, cacophony of bird
Songs at the windows, same old light—
Elpenor, Jesus, Easter every day!

GRAVESTONE INSCRIPTION

STROLLING THIS WAY
DON'T STUDY TO FIT
("NATURE'S FIRST GREEN IS GOLD")
MAKE SOUND ALTERATIONS
("NOTHING GOLD CAN STAY")
AND
SIGN THEM

LATE SHOW

A Muse for Edward Field

Between the shutters, migrate, float
The duck soup at the window now,
Bright horn, top hat blocked by Chagall,
Great baggy, magic overcoat—
Akaky cruising for a mouth?
A mute ghost yet, and hovering
His loud hole in the fog to stare
At mine? Looking for all the world
Like Harpo air-borne by those curls
Only young bards may emulate—
God knows much wiggier than Blake's—
This one's angelic when it clowns
Around. It rolls its sleeves to prove
There's nothing there, then circles in,
Producing with deep care the flask
Which tunes heaven's bright instrument.

SPIRIT DUCK

Named six times without figuring his bill,
Which bounces to his bobbing anyway,
Points him likewise perhaps toward Patrick Spence,
Kidd, or his big pump's downy Beatrice,
Depending on the angles of his dives—
But flesh kept still as tight as hazelnuts.
Beyond the turnstones, bundled on a swell,
Himself between skills, sleepy, measuring
Which wind is going to wind him up today,
Bufflehead pops up on the very top
Of what the British used to call their world,
Balled tiny, cobbycrest, our puppet bird,
Unbaffled by himself the spirit duck.

We meant to be watched too. By Audubon,
Our flying parts, framed also, might put on
Cold earthbound airs to brave the tide-ripped mouth
Of every stream between us and the South.
Much of what's blessed, we pray, rides out the sea.
The rest is your word, I say, about me.

But here's bold dipper, dapper, spirit duck,
Most dear right now of mainly nicknamed things
Because the eye becomes the bouncing mind's
Best caller giving tongue to lesser wings.

Books by Good Deed Rain

Saint Lemonade, Allen Frost, 2014. Two novels illustrated by the author in the manner of the old Big Little Books.

Playground, Allen Frost, 2014. Poems collected from seven years of chapbooks.

Roosevelt, Allen Frost, 2015. A Pacific Northwest novel set in July, 1942, when a boy and a girl search for a missing elephant. Illustrated throughout by Fred Sodt.

5 Novels, Allen Frost, 2015. Novels written over five years, featuring circus giants, clockwork animals, detectives and time travelers.

The Sylvan Moore Show, Allen Frost, 2015. A short story omnibus of 193 stories written over 30 years.

Town in a Cloud, Allen Frost, 2015. A 3-part book of poetry, written during the Bellingham rainy seasons of fall, winter, and spring.

A Flutter of Birds Passing Through Heaven: A Tribute to Robert Sund, 2016. Edited by Allen Frost and Paul Piper. The story of a legendary Ish River poet & artist.

At the Edge of America, Allen Frost, 2016. Two novels in one book blend time travel in a mythical poetic America.

Lake Erie Submarine, Allen Frost, 2016. Two weeks in Ohio inspired these poems, illustrated by the author.

and Light, Paul Piper, 2016. Poetry written over three years. Illustrated with watercolors by Penny Piper.

The Book of Ticks, Allen Frost, 2017. A giant collection of 8 mysterious adventures featuring Phil Ticks. Illustrated throughout by Aaron Gunderson.

I Can Only Imagine, Allen Frost, 2017. Five adventures of love and heartbreak dreamed in an imaginary world. Cover & color illustrations by Annabelle Barrett.

The Orphanage of Abandoned Teenagers, Allen Frost, 2017. A fictional guide for teens and their parents. Illustrated by the author.

In the Valley of Mystic Light: An Oral History of the Skagit Valley Arts Scene, 2017. Edited by Claire Swedberg & Rita Hupy.

Different Planet, Allen Frost, 2017. Four science fiction adventures: reincarnation, robots, talking animals, outer space and clones. Cover & illustrations by Laura Vasyutynska.

Go with the Flow: A Tribute to Clyde Sanborn, 2018. Edited by Allen Frost. The life and art of a timeless river poet.

Homeless Sutra, Allen Frost, 2018. Four stories: Sylvan Moore, a flying monk, a water salesman, and a guardian rabbit.

The Lake Walker, Allen Frost 2018. A little novel set in black and white like one of those old European movies about death and life.

A Hundred Dreams Ago, Allen Frost, 2018. A winter book of poetry and prose. Illustrated by Aaron Gunderson.

Almost Animals, Allen Frost, 2018. A collection of linked stories, thinking about what makes us animals.

The Robotic Age, Allen Frost, 2018. A vaudeville magician and his robot track down ghosts. Illustrated throughout by Aaron Gunderson.

Kennedy, Allen Frost, 2018. This sequel to Roosevelt is a coming-of-age fable set during two weeks in 1962 in a mythical Kennedy-land. Illustrated throughout by Fred Sodt.

Fable, Allen Frost, 2018. There's something going on in this country and I can best relate it in fable: the parable of the rabbits, a bedtime story, and the diary of our trip to Ohio.

Elbows & Knees: Essays & Plays, Allen Frost, 2018. A thrilling collection of writing about some of my favorite subjects, from B-movies to Brautigan.

The Last Paper Stars, Allen Frost 2019. A trip back in time to the 20 year old mind of Frankenstein, and two other worlds of the future.

Walt Amherst is Awake, Allen Frost, 2019. The dreamlife of an office worker. Illustrated throughout by Aaron Gunderson.

When You Smile You Let in Light, Allen Frost, 2019. An atomic love story in NYC.

Pinocchio in America, Allen Frost, 2019. After 82 years buried underground, Pinocchio is resurrected in America.

Taking Her Sides on Immortality, Robert Huff, 2019. The long awaited poetry collection from a local, nationally renowned master of words.

Auld Lang Syne

When I see Aphrodite's locks
Curled above Mae's glad rage—
Especially when Mae's elbowing
Between two crying jags

And Joe behind the bar can tell
How long she'll bawl and beg
Before she smears my handkerchief,
Perks up, pats at my leg,

Whispers aloud: "Only as old
As what the heart reveals..."
I know if we have one more Scotch
I'll slip back where it feels

Autumnal on the campus, green
To orange, rust, a psalm
Hovering in the elms which shade
Professor L. Kirschbaum,

Who waddled into Annex A
That post-war, amber year
Platoons of wrinkled freshmen troops
Signed up to read Shakespeare

And found Professor Leo set
The Quonset hut aglow
To illustrate that pound for pound,
Pricked, prime tongue's heady flow

Sizes the blood more cuttingly
Than beans picked row by row.
Thus he compared Avon's sweet bard
To Walden Pond's Thoreau.

Round Leo Kirschbaum's is the kind
Of memory one keeps.
In time with Hopkins' tearful child,
I listen. Leo weeps

For Hector's fate, for Antony's,
The grief of aged Lear;
For Sam, who fell for altitude
And failed to soar, Sam's tear.

For Leo I shall mourn again
After that closing round
Mae rambles toward so faithfully
Is but a tinkling sound

Circling its vibrations through
Muddled, thin memory:
Lost Sam aloft earthward in air
Outplummeting Mae, me,

Beyond sad Leo's choky sobs
Making their ghostly breeze,
Filling the winds sailing around
Fair Aphrodite's knees.

Robert Huff